Harm-Less Lawsuits?

AEI LIABILITY STUDIES
Michael S. Greve
Series Editor

The AEI Liability Studies examine aspects of the U.S. civil liability system central to the political debates over liability reform. Individual studies analyze the consequences of important liability doctrines for consumer welfare and productive efficiency, assess the effectiveness of recently enacted liability reforms, examine intricate jurisdictional and institutional dilemmas, and propound original proposals for improvement. The goal of the series is to contribute new empirical evidence and promising reform ideas that are commensurate to the seriousness of America's liability problems.

HARM-LESS LAWSUITS?
WHAT'S WRONG WITH CONSUMER CLASS ACTIONS
Michael S. Greve

Harm-Less Lawsuits?

What's Wrong with Consumer Class Actions

Michael S. Greve

The AEI Press

Publisher for the American Enterprise Institute

WASHINGTON, D.C.

2005

Available in the United States from the AEI Press, c/o Client Distribution Services, 193 Edwards Drive, Jackson, TN 38301. To order, call toll free: 1-800-343-4499. Distributed outside the United States by arrangement with Eurospan, 3 Henrietta Street, London WC2E 8LU, England.

Library of Congress Cataloging-in-Publication Data
Greve, Michael S.
    Harm-less lawsuits? what's wrong with consumor class actions / Michael S. Greve.
        p. cm.
Includes bibliographical references.
    ISBN 0-8447-4215-5 (pbk. : alk paper)
        1. Consumer protection—Law and legislation—United States.
2. Consumer protection—Law and legislation—Economic aspects—United States. 3. Class actions (Civil procedure)—United States.
4. Class actions (Civil procedure)—Economic aspects—United States.
I. Title.

    KF1609.G745. 2005
    343.7307'1—dc22

                                                2005004123

    10 09 08 07 06 05 04   1 2 3 4 5 6 7

Cover photograph: Supreme Court building exterior, Washington D.C.

Printed in the United States of America

Contents

Foreword

The "liability explosion" would be much easier to address if it were in fact, as the term implies, a sudden event with a specific cause. But the expansion of legal liability beyond its traditional common-law boundaries has been a gradual, evolutionary process, with numerous interwoven causes. For example, until a century ago tort cases were, for the most part, disputes between citizens of the same political jurisdiction, decided by local judges and juries. With the emergence of large corporations and the growth of interstate commerce, tort cases increasingly pitted local plaintiffs against out-of-state citizens or corporations with highly diffused ownership—but were still decided by judges and juries of the plaintiffs' states or communities, whose tendency to dispense justice with more attentive sympathy for neighbor-plaintiffs than for foreigner-defendants was strong and systematic. Beneficial economic developments produced an unfortunate byproduct: the transformation of a system of dispute resolution into the unconstrained imposition of a tort tax.

The progressive expansion of liability had many political, intellectual, and even cultural causes in addition to economic ones. Although many changes in legal doctrines and procedures were reasonable adaptations to social change, by the end of the twentieth century the system as a whole was producing many results that were manifestly unjust, socially harmful, and economically counterproductive. Still, the movement for legal reform was as slow and complex as the phenomena it responded to. Not only had freewheeling liability produced a politically powerful interest group adamantly opposed to reform—the trial lawyers—but the liability system itself was highly decentralized, with many subtle features and interdependent parts. Many proposals to improve it by revising one or another legal rule foundered on the problem of top-down regulation: Revising a single feature of a complex system leads the other features to respond in kind, which may leave matters even worse than they were before. Only in recent years, a quarter-century after the liability explosion first attracted political notice, have state and federal reforms begun to appear with serious evidence or prospects of yielding tangible improvements.

The problems of excessive legal liability have been a longstanding concern of the American Enterprise Institute. In this monograph series, AEI aims to inform the growing political debates with original, intellectually rigorous research and scholarship by some of America's leading students of law and economics. Series editor Michael S. Greve, who is John G. Searle Scholar at AEI, is himself a leading thinker and writer as well as an activist in liability-reform circles. The studies presented here aim to be attuned to the strengths as well as deficiencies of our civil liability system, and to address the most serious issues in the policy debates. Some contributions supply much-needed empirical data and analysis, while others tackle the intricate institutional problems of the civil justice system. Above all, the studies aim to contribute fresh ideas and practical reform proposals that are commensurate to the depth and gravity of the problem of unbounded liability.

CHRISTOPHER DEMUTH
President
American Enterprise Institute
for Public Policy Research

Acknowledgments

The author is indebted to Michael Petrino and Kate Rick for capable research assistance and to Jack Calfee, Chris DeMuth, Richard Epstein, Robert Gasaway, Eric Helland, Michael Kelly, Jonathan Klick, Francis McGovern, David Rosenberg, and Paul Rubin for helpful comments on an earlier draft.

Portions of the text appeared in a more technical version entitled "Consumer Law, Class Actions, and the Common Law," in *Chapman Law Review* 7 (2004): 155–79.

Introduction

Until very recently, American tort law operated on the ancient maxim of "no harm, no foul." Plaintiffs in search of damages or other relief had to show that they suffered some tangible injury as a consequence of the defendant's conduct. That is no longer so. A 2003 state court verdict in a class-action suit styled *Price v. Philip Morris* attracted much press attention on account of its remarkable size—$10.1 *billion*.[1] Much less noted was the fact that the action presented no claim of past, present, or future smoking-related injury. The class of plaintiffs consisted entirely of smokers who complained about, and recovered damages for, the defendants' allegedly deceptive advertising of "light" and "low-tar" cigarettes (which were marketed in meticulous compliance with federal warning requirements). Personal injury claims were specifically preserved; that is, members of the *Price* class, or for that matter any other consumers of the products, may continue to sue over such harms.

Price is the proverbial tip of the iceberg. Contemporary consumer class actions often dispense with an injury requirement or, more precisely, with a "reliance" element that connects the plaintiffs' alleged losses to the defendants' alleged misdeeds.[2] In a raft of cases involving computer software, pharmaceuticals, automobiles, insurance policies, and other products, plaintiffs' attorneys have demanded, and sometimes obtained, billion-dollar verdicts over alleged corporate misrepresentations even where the plaintiff class consisted predominantly, and often exclusively, of individuals whose harms were purely hypothetical.

The idea of compensating unharmed individuals conflicts with elementary intuitions about the nature and purposes of a legal

1

system. Tort law, we ordinarily believe, should deter wrongful conduct and compensate harmed individuals. To be sure, "wrongs" and "harms" are malleable concepts, and during the course of the twentieth century, civil-liability and, especially, products-liability law underwent a dramatic expansion. Tort law replaced contract law as the basic source of liability. Traditional, liability-limiting tort doctrines (for example, consideration of a purchaser's "contributory negligence" in causing an accident) were weakened and, in the early 1960s, virtually abolished.[3]

Even so, it seems a quantum leap from expanded liability to the infliction of liability where no harm has been done to the plaintiffs. Surely, such "harm-less" lawsuits are aberrant horror stories from the frontiers of our dysfunctional tort system. If that were so, the appropriate reform agenda would be to pursue "tort reform" with renewed vigor. Unfortunately, however, class actions on behalf of unharmed consumers are not simply an excess or aberration. They are quite common, and they result from a confluence of potent political and intellectual forces that are not easily stemmed or reversed.

As a political, institutional matter, harm-less lawsuits rest in large measure on *statutory* law—typically, general-purpose provisions against consumer fraud, unfair business practices, and the like. Obviously, those laws were enacted by legislatures, not courts. They reflect an ambitious and hugely successful attempt to establish a freestanding body of "consumer law," separate and apart from the common-law rules that traditionally governed relations between the sellers and buyers of consumer goods. The obvious implication, widely ignored by tort reformers, is that statutory law, as well as judge-made liability rules, may need reform. Pulling at one string or the other may only produce a tighter knot. Intellectually, harm-less lawsuits rest not simply on antibusiness nostrums, but also on an imposing body of law and economics scholarship. In some versions, that scholarship yields theorems that are congruent with an ideological consumer law, and strikingly at odds with more traditional common-law ideas.

The confluence of institutional and intellectual forces that has produced harm-less lawsuits implies that a serious reform effort will have to be broader, and will be substantially more difficult, than any conventional tort-reform agenda. This monograph seeks to make a start. Its central point is that harm-less class actions, *on top of existing protections for injured consumers*, punish corporate defendants twice for the same conduct. As Judge Frank Easterbrook of the Seventh Circuit Court of Appeals has put it, "If tort law fully compensates those who are physically injured, then any recoveries by those whose products function properly means excess compensation."[4] In allowing both types of suits (without one foreclosing the other), we have two liability regimes operating on top of one another, over the same range of transactions. Such a dual regime is bound to deter a wide range of productive activity, without serving a sensible public purpose.

The problem can be addressed by choosing one legal regime to the exclusion of the other, or by coordinating the regimes so as to minimize the conflicts and inefficiencies. Either course of action would benefit from a better understanding of the origins and the nature of the problem. Thus, the analysis begins by describing the origin of harm-less class actions as part of an ideologically conceived "consumer law" (part I), and then turns to the perplexing support for that construct in parts of the law and economics literature (part II). Readers with a low tolerance for theoretical discussions may wish to turn directly to parts III–V, which discuss the practical difficulties of harm-less class actions and the prospects for reform.

I

The Consumer Law of the Horse

Suppose (a well-worn but instructive hypothetical story runs) a gentleman intent on entering the horse trade were to ask his lawyer for advice on the legal landscape. Would a competent counsel perform a Westlaw search for every case with a mention of "horse"? Or would he advise the entrepreneur of the basics of contracts and torts, even at some risk of underinclusiveness (leaving out, say, some obscure precedent involving carcass disposal in Iowa) and overinclusiveness (such as bringing in liability precedents involving automobiles)? Not even close. The horse trader's transactions are easily captured under the traditional doctrines of contracts and torts, and they are comprehensible only in the broader context of commercial law. The implied terms of contracts in the horse market will differ from those in the markets for airplanes or avocados, but the structural issues are the same. This explains why there is no distinct "law of the horse."[5]

The absurdity of equine law also explains why the call for some new, separate body of law typically rests on a claim that some transactions are wholly unlike those contemplated by the common law. Antitrust law has become an established body of law because we believe that certain contracts—those in restraint of trade—should not only be unenforceable but affirmatively prohibited. Other transitions to new legal arrangements break with common-law notions for overtly ideological reasons. In the 1930s, common-law doctrines governing relations between employers and employees were trumped by "labor law," meaning the law of labor unions and collective bargaining, on the theory that individual workers were powerless against corporate employers. Three decades later, "employment law" was superimposed on preexisting layers of employment-at-will and collective bargaining rights—this time to empower minority workers against racist employers *and* unions. Those bodies of law cover the same transactions; they differ chiefly with respect to the underlying presumptions.[6]

In the same fashion, "consumer law"—unknown before the 1970s—does not cover a single transaction that is not also covered by traditional common-law doctrines. Handbooks and treatises often define consumer law in contradistinction to commercial law—that is, the law governing transactions among merchants.[7] The common law, of course, made no such distinction; it rested on a robust, across-the-board presumption in favor of freedom of contract. Even the Uniform Commercial Code treats, with rare exceptions, consumer transactions under the same rules that apply to comparable business transactions.

Consumer-law advocates, however, insist that the assumptions that underpin freedom of contract do not obtain in the context of consumer transactions. In often colorful language, consumer lawyers paint a picture of ignorant, impulsive consumers who stumble helplessly through a world of corporate monopolies.[8] In soberer moments, they identify the characteristics that supposedly distinguish consumer markets: asymmetric information between producers and consumers (or wholesale consumer ignorance); unequal bargaining power; irrational consumer preferences. Consumer law attempts to redress these problems by imposing affirmative disclosure obligations; through outright prohibitions on abusive, extortionate, or unconscionable contract terms and sales practices; or through mandatory cooling-off or revocation periods.

Changed presumptions produce changed legal rules. Where tort law required an actual injury as an essential element of a cause of action, consumer law dispenses with that and related requirements. Where the common law matched the seller's duty to steer clear of fraud and misrepresentation with the contractual principle of "buyer beware," consumer law imposes a unilateral duty of disclosure on the seller.

Upon inspection, these rationalizations prove too much or too little to define a discrete field of "consumer law." Information is asymmetric in business as well as consumer transactions (the seller often knows more than the buyer); still, for good reasons, the general rule remains "buyer beware." Bargaining power is often unequal in the business sector, but within the general framework of protections against fraud and monopoly, we let parties deal, or not deal, as they wish. (We do not enact statutes to protect Wal-Mart's suppliers, for instance.) Modern behavioral economists have advanced considerably beyond the often crude and occasionally crackpot theories that informed the expansion of liability and the creation of consumer law four decades ago.[9] Still, evidence of pervasive irrationality is far too conjectural to warrant careless paternalism. At most, it may justify circumspect interventions that protect the irrational from costly mistakes without, in the process, inflicting excessive costs on the rational.[10] There is, then, no set of criteria or principles that reliably delineates a discrete consumer law.

The attempt to conjure up such a body of law partook of a broader, explicitly ideological reform movement. Beginning in the 1960s, policy advocates and legal scholars argued that common-law forms and formalities were an impediment to social reform, to the effective management of public problems, and to the aspirations and interests of deserving political constituencies. At its zenith, this critique became distilled in an ambitious effort to develop a full-blown theory of "public law," in contradistinction to "private" or common law.[11] The venue for the most serious and thoroughgoing version of this argument was environmental law, whose champions claimed that environmental complexities rendered common-law distinctions between "mine" and "thine" a menace to an imperiled planet. In an interconnected world, human activities become per se externalities; when an endangered woodpecker decides to build its nest where you want to build your house, the bird wins, and you lose.[12] The ambition of environmental law to manage entire ecosystems in accordance with a coherent political scheme implies a full-scale repudiation of the common law and its theoretical foundations, including notions of property, harm, or individual injury.

Consumer-law advocates initially rested their case on a more modest critique of the common law and of a market economy. Affirmative-disclosure obligations, they argued, would make for more informed consumers and hence better customers. They would not stifle but rather improve competition. Unlike environmental law, then, consumer law remained at least superficially tied to the realities of production and markets. (In fact, federal and state prohibitions against unfair trade practices, beginning with the Federal Trade Commission Act in 1915, were originally intended to protect competitors, not consumers.) Instead of attacking the common law at its roots, advocates could plausibly rest their case on the enforcement problems and transaction costs of common-law litigation.

The argument (as we shall see, an important point of contact and congruence between consumer law and law and economics scholarship) is that victims of wrongful conduct are often precluded from asserting their claims, especially when—as is often the case in consumer transactions—those claims are small, or the costs of proving them are high. (For example, fraud cases require proof of the defendant's knowing and intentional misrepresentation.) The costs of detecting and proving unlawful conduct may further exacerbate a tendency toward underenforcement and underdeterrence. That is especially so when even the full enforcement of the available remedies—such as damages under the out-of-pocket rule, which limits the plaintiff's monetary recovery to his actual losses—leaves a lawbreaking defendant no worse off (net of the costs of defending the claims) than his law-abiding competitor.

This emphasis on the deficiencies of common-law adjudication suggests plausible remedies short of establishing an independent body of consumer law. An obvious choice is to entrust public agencies with the definition and enforcement of injunctions against unfair or fraudulent business practices without having to prove the common-law elements, such as the defendant's intent to deceive. Another strategy is to jack up the rewards for private enforcers. (Antitrust law, for example, offers treble damages to prevailing plaintiffs.) A third strategy is the bundling of small consumer claims in class actions. While all three strategies predate the invention of modern consumer law by a half-century, their use increased enormously during the 1970s, when Congress and state legislatures enacted a raft of consumer-protection statutes. Statutory damages provisions and jury awards proliferated. And, in the wake of the 1966 class-action reforms, federal and state courts created a novel and remarkably permissive regime for the prosecution and adjudication of mass claims.

That accommodation of perceived consumer needs, though, failed to create an equilibrium where consumer law could come to rest. It is exceedingly difficult to tailor private rewards to deterrence objectives; in any event, their effectiveness still depends on entrepreneurial trial lawyers and on the availability of a sufficiently large plaintiff class. Government consumer-protection agencies, even when run by consumer advocates, still operate under budgetary constraints and countervailing political pressures. Modern class actions are fraught with problems, from exorbitant transaction costs to the possibility of "sweetheart" settlements that dilute the deterrent value of such actions. (When hit with a mass of identical class actions, corporate defendants often attempt to hold a "reverse auction" among plaintiffs' lawyers and to strike a preclusive settlement with the attorney who will sell the class claims for the least amount of money.)[13]

Besides, consumer law itself creates an upward demand spiral. Confronted with a prohibition against competition on some margin (for example, interest rates on consumer loans or mortgages), sellers will compete on some other, less transparent margin, thus creating demands for additional interventions.[14] So: Should one go farther? On consumerist premises, of course one should. If more laws and affirmative obligations, bigger government agencies and enforcement budgets, and better incentives for injured consumers don't do the job, the natural move is to mimic environmental law after all: Divorce the definition of torts from individual harm, legal claims from their common-law owners, and legal theories from production values.

Environmental law starts with transcendental public values ("species protection") and then mobilizes private-law forms to vindicate the values, as when an endangered bird wings its way into a federal courtroom, accompanied by a trustworthy guardian from the Sierra Club Legal Defense Fund. Consumer law, perhaps because it must start with actual people rather than transcendental concerns, reached its destination from the opposite direction. It gradually slipped its harm-based moorings and finally arrived at what a leading advocate of mass tort actions (David Rosenberg) has called a "public-law" version of torts.[15] Its point is to achieve tort law's public purpose, which is to promote consumer interests through the optimal deterrence of corporate misconduct. On that theory, liability need not be predicated on a connection between a defendant's misconduct and the plaintiff's harm. We should in all events be grateful that *someone*, injured or not, comes forward to deter misconduct.

II

Efficient Consumer Class Actions?

The ideological movement that produced harm-less class actions has received potent support from leading law and economics scholars— who are devoted to economic efficiency rather than consumerism per se, much less transcendentalism, and who are widely suspected of corporate sympathies. Although law and economics paradigms hardly compel an endorsement of every facet of consumer law (including harm-less class actions), the basic presumptions are largely congruent. Most important, both camps share an aversion to contracts, as opposed to torts. Consumer advocates wear that disdain on their shirtsleeves; their entire movement rests on the notion that consumer contracts are a means of exploitation. Many economists seriously doubt that premise, and some leading scholars have made a powerful case for contracts, rather than torts, as an efficient means of handling many liability problems.[16] In other versions, however, law and economics scholarship improbably converges on Naderite nostrums.

A prime example is *Making Tort Law*, by Charles Fried and David Rosenberg, a sophisticated but readily understandable economic approach to tort law.[17] Consistent with the great body of law and economics scholarship, Fried and Rosenberg argue that an efficient liability system should focus on creating optimal incentives to deter harmful conduct, rather than compensating accident victims after the fact. The deterrence function of tort law is often (though somewhat misleadingly) called the "insurance function," because the efficient deterrence level is a function of the costs and the likelihood of an accident—in other words, the level of insurance that rational, risk-averse, fully informed consumers would purchase.[18] In addition, tort law serves to compensate the victims of wrongful conduct. But that purpose is secondary to deterrence, because compensation can be achieved more readily and far more cheaply through insurance.[19]

Fried and Rosenberg inveigh against commingling questions of compensation and deterrence, arguing that a failure to separate them will produce poor results. For example, the appropriate amount of compensation for individual plaintiffs will often depend on such factors as a class member's degree of fault or negligence in contributing to an accident or on the availability of third-party insurance. But those considerations, Fried and Rosenberg argue (not altogether convincingly), have nothing to do with the optimal deterrence award.[20] Judges should first calculate what the defendant should pay and only then, and separately, determine what individual class members should receive from the common pool.[21]

At the limit, this model pushes toward mandatory class actions— that is, plaintiff classes that contain every conceivable claimant, without providing an opportunity to opt out of the class.[22] That is so because an injured party's opt-out is very likely an opportunistic attempt to collect more, by way of damages, than the amount for which a rational, risk-averse individual would have insured prior to the accident. For analogous reasons, the model implies an endorsement of harm-less lawsuits. The useful function performed by plaintiffs (or for that matter by entrepreneurial lawyers) is to bring a matter before a court for the determination of an appropriate deterrence award. For that purpose, it is irrelevant whether the class includes or even consists entirely of unharmed plaintiffs. The harms, to repeat, have to do not with deterrence but with compensation. Courts should address the deterrence question first. There will be time enough to weed out unharmed claimants at a later stage.

Fried and Rosenberg call their model "*ex ante*" because its basic rules derive from a calculation of what sensible members of society would desire before knowing that they have been or will be harmed— rather than after the fact, when they will tend to exaggerate their losses and falsely proclaim ignorance about the risks of the purchased product. This perspective makes eminent sense. It is the starting point of modern social theory from James Buchanan to John Rawls.[23]

On a more practical note, it is the reason for insurance markets, which provide individuals with the opportunity to hedge their bets— to maximize their utility, as economists say more precisely—among various possible states of the world, *before* knowing which of those states will, in fact, occur. The same perspective makes perfect sense in thinking about liability rules, which is why it is common ground in modern tort scholarship.

In some versions, that scholarship has yielded supposedly efficient rules that differ dramatically from more traditional common-law ones. The "decoupling" of compensation from deterrence in the Fried and Rosenberg model, as well as the insistence on mandatory class actions and the notion of unharmed plaintiffs, are examples. That circumstance, plus the characterization of the model as *ex ante*, suggests that the common-law rules of old somehow rested on a different perspective. But that is not so. Contracts, one of the most basic building blocks of the common law, are the quintessential tool of managing risks and assigning liability *ex ante*. In real life, insurance contracts and consumer warranties, among other products, serve this function. In theory, contract law (as well as tort law) attempts to supply legal rules that the parties would have chosen *ex ante* in a world without transaction costs.[24] Private agreements provide the baseline for figuring out how to deal with unallocated losses, not the other way around. Put differently, a theory that attempts to mimic in tort law the rules and arrangements that fully informed, risk-averse consumers *would* have chosen *ex ante* is derivative of contracts. *Making Tort Law* avowedly is such an *ex ante* analysis. And yet, it contains not one word (except by way of disparagement) about contracts.

The point of that striking and fateful departure is captured in Rosenberg's characterization, quoted earlier, of his perspective as a "public-law" theory of torts, as distinct from a traditional "private," or common-law, version. This change in perspective entails two crucial differences. First, the common law viewed torts as part of a private ordering among autonomous individuals. Second, it comprehended torts—not always systematically, but certainly as a matter of basic intuition—in the context of a larger web of private arrangements. The public-law perspective, in contrast, views torts as a public regulatory system, and it tends to isolate that system from its social and legal context.

Private and Public

The essentially "private" perspective of the common law is reflected in the insistence that legal entitlements must belong exclusively to their real-world owners—in contract, to the parties who signed the instrument; in torts, to the parties who were injured (and, in an earlier age, the narrower class of individuals who were in "privity" with the producer of a defective product).[25] This is why individuals generally may not sell their tort claims to third parties and why, conversely, they cannot be made party to a suit without their consent. Public-law theory, in contrast, conceptualizes tort law from the perspective of its public function, which is to maximize social welfare by means of efficient legal rules. From that vantage, there is no a priori reason why legal claims should belong exclusively to their legal owners. We award compensation to individual plaintiffs (rather than having deterrence-inducing payments made to the government) because compensation provides incentives for suit, not because the claims are somehow owned by the plaintiffs. The question of who can sue whom for what is not a matter of indifference, since it is important—and devilishly difficult—to get the enforcement incentives right. Contrary to common-law intuitions, however, there is nothing inherently bizarre about assigning those rights to someone other than, or in addition to, harmed parties.

Context

The private, common-law perspective puts tort liability in a broader context, both with respect to its function and its consequences. Functionally, tort liability is only one of several private and *ex ante* arrangements to deter harmful conduct. First in line is the competitive discipline of private markets. In the ordinary course of business, killing one's customers is not a profit-maximizing strategy, both because the dead are lousy repeat customers and because reputational losses may ruin the business as a going concern. A second line of defense is contracts.

It is only after these defenses have broken down that tort law operates as a deterrent, as a kind of backstop to market pressures and contracts. With respect to consequences, the imposition of common-law liability is predicated on its fit with the larger web of private orderings and its effects on the next set of transactions. The clearest example is the ancient doctrine of *damnum absque injuria*—that is, a harm that is nonetheless not compensable. In an individual case, it may seem tempting and perhaps even "efficient" to impose liability for the very real harms of economic competition, such as closed factories or lost jobs. But that one-shot transaction seems far less desirable from a broader and more dynamic perspective; private orderings would collapse, and the benefits of competition would be lost, if the winners had to compensate the losers. For that reason, competitive harms are the pristine example of *damnum absque injuria.*

The fact that the public-law perspective yields a doctrine, or at least a toleration, of *injuria absque damno*—a recognizable claim without a harm—illustrates the radical shift in outlook. Of course, law and economics scholars know very well that markets and contracts deter much harmful conduct. Due to basic theoretical commitments, however, much of the literature severs tort law from its context and assumes that it acts as the *sole* deterrent of wrongful conduct.[26]

Many law and economics scholars understand tort law as a public and, specifically, a judicial enterprise; regardless of what judges think they are doing, the best understanding of the law flows from the hypothesis that they act *as if* they were engaged in a collective enterprise of efficient resource allocation.[27] If that is right, the broad move from contract to tort over the past century must be approximately efficient. But that supposition is not obviously correct. Proponents of the efficiency view have suggested that such factors as the increased complexity of industrial production or deep-seated psychological biases and their exploitation by corporate producers render consumers incapable of bargaining for efficient liability protections.[28]

When such purported explanations prove unsatisfactory (as they have), the usual theoretical move is a resort to unspecified transaction costs. If the allocation of liability between producers and consumers has become a matter of tort rather than contract, the argument runs, that must be so because the bargaining costs of contractual agreements between buyer and seller are prohibitively high. So crucial a theoretical assumption should be backed by robust empirical evidence. It is not. In fact, there are good reasons to think that contractual bargaining costs have gone down rather than up (for example, through warranties and standardized consumer contracts). And we have persuasive evidence that tort law, rather than contract law, imposes very substantial transaction costs.[29]

Having made the move from contracts to torts, the theorists argue over the efficiency characteristics of particular liability rules—such as "strict liability" versus a "negligence" rule—and attempt to derive optimal deterrence rules under certain well-specified conditions. (Such "possibility theorems" often operate with assumptions of zero transaction costs and zero judicial errors.) The models often yield valuable insights. But if the account of the basic social choice of tort law over contract law is mistaken, the choice of this or that supposedly deterrence-optimizing tort doctrine is an argument over the last 2 percent of (in)efficiency. In any event, the theorems are not robust with respect to their assumptions, so that even a slight change in the assumptions may yield very different results.

For example, the general proposition that tort law should generate optimal incentives *ex ante* yields no agreement on how that might be done. As a first approximation, as noted, *ex ante* theory looks to the losses that rational and risk-averse individuals would have insured prior to the accident. The theory works reasonably well for pecuniary losses, for which there is an actual insurance market that tort law can mimic. It works much less smoothly, and hence commands far less scholarly consensus, for nonpecuniary, pain-and-suffering losses, such as the loss of an infant child—which is very real, but not the type of loss against which people do insure.[30] The answers here hang on highly contestable assumptions.

Writing fifteen years ago, two prominent scholars noted that "a decade of effort by economists to develop theories of tort law succeeded on its own scholarly terms, but economists all too often provided efficiency proofs for institutions that most lawyers now view as inefficient."[31] Stripping tort law from its context has its uses *for analytical purposes*—provided it is accompanied by a recognition of just how far the enterprise takes us from the real world. The extreme assumption that tort law serves as an exclusive deterrent—crucial to the entire enterprise—renders the models more elegant and manageable. But it ought to be accompanied by an acknowledgment that we have strikingly little evidence that tort acts as *a* deterrent, let alone an exclusive one. The authors of one of the rare empirical studies in the field concluded their findings (and an exhaustive literature survey) by observing that "the great disappointment that the deterrent effect of tort is limited and uneven and or cannot be established by existing studies suggests that considerable intellectual effort has been expended on models that omit some crucial facts about the real world, including high transaction costs and imperfect information. . . . [T]heory can take us only so far."[32]

Unless it is handled with care, one might add, theory may take us far down a wrong and unintended path. Harm-less consumer class actions provide a picture-book illustration. The most ardent purveyors of a deterrence-first liability regime (such as Fried and Rosenberg) hold out their model as an *alternative* to more traditional, harm-based legal doctrines—not as a *supplement* to those doctrines. But before jumping from the model to policy prescription, one would like to know a whole lot about how likely its idealized conditions are to obtain in practice—and about the likely results when those conditions do *not* obtain.

And there is the rub. In real life, the old common-law doctrines remain. They resonate with deeply held intuitions about making people whole and letting them have their day in court, and those intuitions are not easily displaced. The creation of a supposedly efficient consumer-law scheme on top of the common law entails a high risk that liability will be inflicted twice—once, to make people whole, and then again, supposedly in the interest of optimal deterrence. Such double recoveries cannot be efficient. Unfortunately, however, they are anything but a theoretical possibility; they have become a common occurrence.

III

Consumer Classes in Action

A simple hypothetical case—based loosely on *Shaw v. Toshiba*, an actual case that eventually settled for a modest $2.1 billion—illustrates the shape and logic of modern consumer class actions.[33] Suppose a company sells a large number of identical computers at a price of $1,000, with a promise (implied or actual) that the product will function flawlessly. Unfortunately, however, it turns out that a series of complex operations, performed by and of use to a very small number of consumers, causes the system to crash. These "marginal" consumers suffer a genuine loss and, but for the manufacturer's misrepresentation, would doubtlessly have purchased a different product. What is the sensible assignment of rights?

The common-law rule, in a nutshell, is to deter negligent misrepresentation or simple mistakes by means of providing redress for those persons, and *only* those persons, who have suffered an injury and, moreover, justifiably relied on the manufacturer's representations. In addition, the plaintiff must show that the representation was, in fact, false and made with the intent of inducing the buyer to rely on it. (Pleading and proof requirements for the historically disfavored tort of fraud are still more demanding.) Plaintiffs who satisfy these requirements may obtain redress under the out-of-pocket rule. Such redress includes restitution for the full purchase price minus the residual value of the product. It also includes the users' opportunity costs—that is, the foregone benefits of purchasing a competing, flawless product.

Most courts now also award so-called "benefit-of-the-bargain" redress for the consumer's disappointed expectations. Under this recovery rule (which was always available in breach-of-contract but only later migrated into torts), courts do not attempt to restore the plaintiff to the position he would have occupied had the misrepresentation never been made; they attempt to put him into the position he would have occupied had the false communication been true.[34] The difference can be quite large.[35] Under either damages rule, however, recovery is limited to the marginal consumers, who satisfy the requirement of detrimental reliance. Inframarginal consumers, for whom the product worked as promised, receive zero compensation. After all, they have already received the full benefit of their bargain—typically including a sizable chunk of consumer surplus, which the buyers will get to keep in any event.[36] The fact that the product failed some *other* purchasers is irrelevant.

The alternative is to run the problem through the public-law model, starting with the question of what legal regime individuals would choose *ex ante*—that is, prior to the purchase, let alone the use, of this or that product. Economic theorists, as noted, argue for a rule that creates adequate deterrence for the manufacturer to make optimal investments in precautions. From this perspective, common-law considerations of injury, inducement, and justifiable reliance are arguably beside the point, and perhaps even harmful. To be sure, if damages are set at the right level, litigation by traditional common-law plaintiffs—the marginal consumers—may produce a deterrence level that will generate optimal investments in precautions. But why should we rely on those consumers and their uncertain incentives to bring suit to extract the seller's windfall? For deterrence purposes, it makes more sense to round up the purchasers all along the demand curve and to figure out the difference between the purchase price and the price that they would have paid, had the true characteristics of the product been known. To be sure, the purchasers will differ greatly with respect to their individual injuries, their reliance on the manufacturer's representation, and other characteristics. But these questions have to do not with the determination of optimal deterrence, but with the *distribution* of the proceeds among plaintiffs. Courts should address those matters after, and separately from, the determination of the correct deterrence level.

As a matter of blackboard theory, it may seem to make little difference whether we exclude the inframarginal consumers—those who do not satisfy detrimental reliance requirements—at the front end or whether we let them tag along as members of a comprehensive class and, at the end of the day, award them zero dollars from the common pool. At least in practice, however, the models are *not* equivalent. Consumer class actions (including some cases of considerable notoriety) that conform to the public-law model push toward an insidious conclusion—a wholesale evisceration of the reliance requirement. A few examples illustrate the pattern:

- *Williams v. Purdue Pharma Co.* was a class action on behalf of purchasers of OxyContin, a potent opioid. The plaintiffs—some 30,000 purchasers—complained that Purdue conducted a deceptive, misleading, and fraudulent advertising campaign, which falsely stated that OxyContin would provide "smooth and sustained pain relief" and, moreover, posed little risk of addiction when used as prescribed. The class plaintiffs did not claim that the product failed to work as advertised *for them* or that *they* became addicted. Instead, they argued that they were deprived of the full benefit of their purchase bargain because the product failed to work as advertised for some *other* consumers. The district court dismissed the claim.[37] Substantially identical class actions, however, remain pending in several states.

- In *Avery v. State Farm Mutual Insurance*, an Illinois jury and judge awarded $1.18 billion to a class of an estimated 4.5 million State Farm customers in forty-eight states whose estimates for auto accident repair costs were assessed by the company on the basis of cheap and allegedly inferior "aftermarket parts" (that is, replacement parts produced by someone other than the original manufacturer).[38] The plaintiffs did not allege that State Farm's policy—which many states encourage or even require so as to control automobile insurance rates—caused them physical injury or consequential pecuniary losses (for example, lost resale value). Instead, they prevailed on the claim that after-market parts are inherently inferior and therefore fail to satisfy State Farm's contractual obligations to restore vehicles to their pre-loss condition.

- In *Price v. Philip Morris*, another Illinois state court approved a $10.1 billion verdict in favor of a class of Illinois purchasers and consumers of Marlboro Lights and Cambridge Lights cigarettes. The action specifically excluded personal injury claims. Instead, plaintiffs claimed that the advertisements of the products as "lights" and "lowered tar and nicotine" were deceptive, unfair, and calculated to create the false impression that the products were safer or less harmful than regular cigarettes. Plaintiffs claimed to have overpaid in reliance on these misrepresentations. They sought and obtained damages for the difference between the purchase price and the value of the product they received. The trial judge credited a consumer survey, conducted by a plaintiff's expert, which estimated the diminution in value at 92.3 percent and, on that basis, arrived at "compensatory" class damages of $7.1 billion. He then complemented the award with punitive damages and attorneys' fees.

- Benefit-of-the-bargain demands on behalf of unharmed parties are not the exclusive province of "hellhole jurisdictions" and rapacious trial lawyers. In March 2000 the FDA asked Warner-Lambert (now owned by Pfizer) to remove the diabetes drug Rezulin from the market because it was responsible for serious and sometimes fatal liver failures. It is uniformly acknowledged that Rezulin, despite its dreadful side effects in some patients, had significant therapeutic benefits for most, and of course, the injured parties (or their estates) are entitled to compensation. In *Desiano v. Warner-Lambert Company*, though, a federal appeals court (Judge Calabresi writing for the court) ruled that *health insurers* may pursue, under New Jersey statutes and common law, claims to recoup the cost of *every* Rezulin prescription filled and reimbursed (minus the patients' copayments) over a four-year period.[39] Warner-Lambert, the theory runs, knowingly made false statements about Rezulin's safety, and the health-care organizations would not have provided the drug or reimbursed their insured customers but for those misrepresentations. On the same theory, it would appear, the insured patients—for the vast majority of whom, to repeat, the drug worked as desired and without adverse effects—would be entitled to recoup their copayments. The plaintiff-companies' damage demand runs to $1.4 billion.

Common-law notions of detrimental reliance and inducement obviously play a distinctly subordinate role in these cases. Otherwise, it is hard to see how a court could possibly certify, *and contemplate compensation for*, inchoate classes of consumers who vary greatly in their degree of reliance and injury (if any).[40]

For what little it is worth, the members of the plaintiff classes described above at least purchased OxyContin, insurance policies, and Marlboro Lights, and they did complain about the characteristics of those products and the sellers' representations. But if we are worried chiefly about deterrence, those limitations, too, may be superfluous. Perhaps *anybody*—including mere bystanders, malcontents, or, for that matter, insurance companies operating at several removes from the allegedly fraudulent transactions—should be permitted to sue and recover damages.

Modern "entrepreneurial" class actions fit this description in all but form: They are instigated and controlled entirely by plaintiffs' lawyers. And at least some courts have explicitly dispensed with the notion that a consumer-plaintiff must have purchased the product in question. For example, the court in *Shaw v. Toshiba* approved a class including *potential* purchasers, on the grounds that "it is not necessary for someone to actually *own* a defective computer in order to experience continuing, adverse effects from it." It was of no consequence "whether Plaintiffs currently own one of Defendants' computers, are thinking about buying one of Toshiba's computers, or are commuting to work over a bridge with design specifications tainted by allegedly faulty [diskette controllers]."[41] From a consumer-law perspective, this seemingly bizarre position is quite plausible.

Statutory law has moved in the same direction. Most prominently, California's Unfair Competition Law (UCL)—commonly known as "Section 17200," its number in the California Business and Professional Code—prohibits "any unlawful, unfair or fraudulent business act or practice and unfair, deceptive, untrue or misleading advertising." "Unlawful" acts are those that are unlawful under any statute; hence, the UCL sweeps across the entire California Code (including the criminal code).[42] Moreover, compliance with the law is not necessarily a defense, since business practices that are not "unlawful" may still be "unfair."[43]

The breathtaking breadth of the UCL was matched until very recently by the liberality of its enforcement provisions. In November 2004, the California voters approved "Proposition 64," a measure that limits the private enforcement of the UCL to plaintiffs who have sustained an actual injury. Previously, the act could be enforced by state and local prosecutors and by literally any private party acting "for the interests of itself, its members or the general public." Anybody could sue anyone else; the only standing requirement was that the plaintiff could effectively represent the broader group's interests. With respect to fraudulent business practices, for example, it was unnecessary to show deception, reasonable reliance, or damages to anybody, let alone the plaintiff.[44] Private enforcement could proceed even where the predicate statute manifestly contemplated no such thing.[45]

In its pre-2004 version, Section 17200 contained none of the ordinary procedural and due-process safeguards of federal class actions, such as notification of absent class members and an opportunity to opt out of a class. Consistent with the logic of the deterrence perspective—which, as suggested earlier, treats the due process–based protections of formal class actions, especially their opt-out provisions, as an invitation to opportunism—Section 17200 actions on behalf of the public could proceed without conforming to federal or state class-action requirements. And while private litigants could not sue for damages under Section 17200, they could obtain injunctive relief, including restitution and disgorgement under equitable principles. The California courts created multiple vehicles to facilitate generous monetary relief. In short, prior to the enactment of Proposition 64, "[t]he only apparent limitation upon the practical reach of the UCL [was] the imagination of man (and woman)."[46]

The best-known UCL plaintiff was Marc Kasky, a self-proclaimed activist who sued Nike over the company's allegedly false statements concerning its corporate practices in third-world countries. Mr. Kasky did not rely on those statements, and certainly not to his detriment. There was no evidence that he had ever purchased a Nike product, and, in any event, the company's communications concerned its employment practices, not the attributes of its sneakers. Nonetheless, and despite Nike's vociferous First Amendment objections, the California Supreme Court permitted the case to go to trial. After an unsuccessful petition to the United States Supreme Court, the case settled for a $1.5 million payment to a corporate watchdog group and Nike's promises to mend its ways, employment- and speech-wise.[47]

One can think of *Kasky v. Nike* as the ultimate consumer class action. Alternatively, one can think of the case as a kind of consumerist public-law action for the production of a more "republican" globalization discourse, which ought to proceed regardless of what millions of real-world citizens and consumers may actually want to hear or say.[48] At this point of perfect convergence between private and public law, consumer law has reached its culmination.

IV

The Harms of Harm-Less Lawsuits

It is true that common-law adjudication may present serious deterrence and transaction-cost problems. It may even be true, as consumer advocates insist, that those problems are particularly pronounced in the context of consumer transactions. The divestiture of legal claims from their common-law owners, however, begets other, potentially far more vexing difficulties. Those difficulties are easily summarized: While the public law, deterrence-first model aims to preclude opportunistic compensation claims, it may in practice greatly *increase* the risk that such claims will be made and be compensated. The likely result is massive overdeterrence.

Due Process

The purpose of tort litigation, according to public-law theory, is to get the deterrence level right. That purpose would be defeated if plaintiffs could sue repeatedly over the same violations. In other words, a deterrence-based regime requires ancillary rules—"preclusion" rules, in legal parlance—that bar multiple or repeat lawsuits. What, then, are those rules?

Mandatory class actions, coupled with a wholesale preclusion of future lawsuits over the same conduct, hold some attraction; they promise to rope all possible claimants into a once-and-for-all determination of the optimal deterrence award. But that regime raises numerous practical problems—prominent among them, the specter that corporate defendants will cut themselves cheap, collusive settlements with a plaintiffs' lawyer of their choice. The problem appears in sharper relief outside the context of formal class actions and their protections for absent class members. Under California's old UCL, as noted, verdicts obtained by private litigants on behalf of the public had no preclusive effect (barring a judgment in a parallel class action). Any such effect would render a statute facially unconstitutional, since it would create a roving commission to dispose of the rights of absent, unnotified parties. But now, the due-process problem appears at the other end: the lack of preclusion raises the very real threat of multiple prosecutions and verdicts over the same violations, by the same parties. The dilemma, which even the California courts have recognized, has no obvious solution.[49]

Excess Payments

Under a "deterrence-first" tort scheme, damage awards will often exceed the plaintiff class's economic losses.[50] First, the "right" level of deterrence will have to account, by means of some multiplier, for the risk that consumers might not detect the offense or sue over it. Second, the *distribution* of damage awards that have been set at an efficient level will take account of common-law defenses (such as a particular plaintiff's contributory negligence or lack of reliance) that will tend to reduce individual plaintiffs' damages. Thus, after the court has provided full insurance compensation for the consumer class, some funds will remain. Where should they go?

Defenders of a deterrence-first regime suggest that judges should dedicate the difference to some "public use."[51] That cheerful appellation falsely suggests that the "public use" is *ipso facto* superior to the producer's alternative private use—including, presumably, investments from retained earnings and the production of future goods or services. (Consumer class-action awards are typically paid not by some robber baron, but by productive enterprises with consumers, shareholders, workers, and a product line with substantial consumer demand and benefits.) Put differently, a transfer that may look efficient in a one-shot, static deterrence model may prove quite inefficient from a broader, dynamic, and, therefore, more realistic perspective. The problem is aggravated when the "excess" is handed over, as in practice it often is, to legal-aid organizations with the stated objective of siphoning off the *next* producer's surplus.[52]

Errors

"Look," public-law theorists argue, "no one seriously doubts that tort law ought to optimize deterrence. That being so, we ought to choose a model that promises to minimize opportunistic compensation claims, transaction costs, and judicial error." On those dimensions, the argument continues, the deterrence-first model gets the nod. Drumming potential claimants into a compulsory class is far cheaper and easier than haggling over entitlements to damages at the preliminary (class-certification) stage. Distribution of the proceeds over a large, heterogeneous class will pose problems; but then, liability awards are always a matter of statistics. Sophisticated survey and sampling techniques will reduce the room for error, and eliminating confusing questions of individual causation or reliance from the deterrence calculations will generate judicial economies of scale.[53] Practical considerations and empirical evidence, however, provide no grounds for such comforting assurances.

Putting compensation first, or commingling it with deterrence questions, may indeed invite damage demands in excess of the amounts for which the claimants would have insured *ex ante*. But that danger is balanced by countervailing considerations. A focus on compensation early in the proceedings implies an inquiry into whether *these* particular claimants are entitled to it—in other words, into questions of detriment, reliance, and the like. The public-law notion that these considerations are a mere distraction from calculating the appropriate deterrence award is gravely mistaken. Pushing questions of injury and reliance off into a later compensation stage compels an abstract inquiry into what an enormously heterogeneous class of claimants *would* have done under conditions of perfect information. That inquiry, outside the context of particularized injuries and questions of reliance, poses great risks of judicial error. It is by definition *ex post*, and the claimants have every reason to lie.

All else being equal, "deterrence-first" expands not simply the size of the plaintiff class but also, and more fatefully, its heterogeneity. That alone induces error. In the *Avery* litigation, the plaintiffs' expert estimated consequential losses—principally, the cost of replacing the installed aftermarket parts with the original manufacturers' products—at anywhere between $658 million and $1.2 billion. On cross-examination, he conceded that his high-end estimate might be off by, oh, $1 billion.[54] Putting aside that rounding error, the expert's calculation treated the car-buff owner of a vintage Corvette (who suffered a genuine loss because he and his potential customers can tell a replacement fender from the real thing) on par with the owner of a run-of-the-mill vehicle with a previously dented fender—who may well be better off because the "inferior" replacement part is superior to the dented, pre-loss original, and because he benefits (as a repeat customer) from State Farm's general aftermarket parts policy.

Likewise, the class in *Price* includes everyone from hypothetical, health-conscious nicotine addicts who believed they were consuming a "safe" product to the merely image-conscious who are under no such illusion and who smoke lights because they are socially more acceptable than in-your-face, filterless Camels. By the *Price* plaintiffs' own lights (no pun intended), there is no such thing as a "safe" cigarette. We are nonetheless asked to believe that one can somehow estimate a demand curve that slopes from here to there. In both *Avery* and *Price*, the courts made do with an expert's wild guess about the margin—*and then effectively treated every claimant as a marginal purchaser.* Putting aside the actual marginal customers (who are bound to be few in *Avery* and nonexistent in *Price*), the claimants are being treated, yet again and by means of a liability verdict, to the benefits of a bargain they have already received.

The lack of direct evidence on the location of the margin or the distribution of claimants along the demand curve would invite this kind of shortcut even if no one had an interest in prompting it. But, of course, plaintiffs have precisely that interest. The insurers' $1.4 billion claim in *Desanio* implies that the Rezulin demand, but for the manufacturer's misrepresentations, would have been nil. In light of Rezulin's massive health benefits for the vast majority of consumers, that contention seems preposterous. The survey relied on in *Price* asked consumers what they would have paid had they known the true nature of the product, and the answer was 7.7 cents on the dollar. (The award is the aggregate difference between that hypothetical price and an allegedly promised "safe" cigarette.) In other words, the respondents all lied.

Of course, courts need not credit such opportunistic averments. But the potential error here runs in only one direction. In consumer class actions—which turn on claims of misrepresentation and the like, rather than bodily harm—the real danger is not so much that claimants will opportunistically exaggerate their harms (which are often ascertainable). The principal risk is that they will inflate the extent of their *reliance*. *Ex post*, all of us are inclined to ascribe a lack of foresight, or the deliberate assumption of a risk, or sheer stupidity, to a lack of information or to misrepresentation. Barring an examination of compensation claims at the front end, the only tolerably safe test of such representations is a counterfactual scenario showing what rational, risk-averse consumers in fact do under conditions of full information. Such scenarios are hard to come by, and not much sought after.[55]

To bring the crucial error to the point: To decouple deterrence from compensation is to decouple it from reliance, causation, and related doctrines that tie the plaintiffs' losses to the defendants' alleged misdeeds. If the earlier case examples do not show why that is, in fact, an error, the much-publicized investigation and prosecution of brokerage firms in the aftermath of the 2001 stock market collapse should provide a further demonstration.

Prior to the crash, brokerage firms published research reports that contained, along with much useful and otherwise unavailable information on covered companies, transaction recommendations for the stocks of those companies. As advertised, the recommendations ranked from "buy" to "sell"; in practice, the firms never issued a recommendation lower than "hold." Nobody batted an eye when the market went up; when it tanked, investors lost their shirts and, predictably, claimed to have been injured by the brokers' "misleading" buy/sell recommendations. Stipulate that the "misleading" characterization is accurate: What is the appropriate deterrence award? And would the estimate benefit from evidence of the extent to which investors relied on the recommendations?

Suppose (to take the limiting case) that, first, "hyping" was a general and widely known industry practice and, second, that all of the brokers' customers knew how to separate the hype from the useful information. In *that* world, early attention to common-law requirements of inducement and reliance would play an indispensable role in determining the appropriate deterrence award—*which might well be zero*.[56] Senior District Judge Pollack of the Southern District of New York roundly dismissed a massive class action against Merrill Lynch in a harshly worded opinion. That ruling flowed unmistakably from the judge's close, upfront scrutiny of the common-law elements of the plaintiffs' fraud claims, from reliance to loss causation.[57] Run the same case through a deterrence-first model, and the likely result (and along with it the settlement incentives) will look very different. The judge will first look to the existence of "misrepresentations," "conflicts of interest," and the like. Having found such infractions (by stipulation), the judge is highly unlikely to conclude that the appropriate deterrence award is zero—even if the investor-plaintiffs' losses were caused in their entirety by the market collapse, rather than the brokers' hype. Perhaps a deterrence award could include some adjustment for lack of reliance (just as awards should include adjustments for the likelihood of detection). Strictly speaking, however, deterrence-first forbids that adjustment, since reliance (under that model) has to do with compensation rather than deterrence. And even if such an adjustment were made, it would suffer from the near-impossibility, noted earlier, of estimating its proper magnitude in the absence of concrete evidence.[58]

At the end of the day, the hoped-for separation of confounding compensation questions from deterrence is a chimera. Postpone compensation questions until the distribution stage, and the process translates into claims on a common pool in whose distribution the judge and the defendants—parties with a stake in considering those questions at an earlier stage—no longer have a serious interest. In practice, the distribution is often performed by independent boards or experts (under general judicial supervision). But that process suffers from an indelible dissonance.[59] In one sense, the "deterrence-first" model urges a serious consideration of individual compensation; its whole point is to weed out opportunistic claims. In another sense, the model treats compensation claims with utter indifference. If reliance, inducement, and the like were truly important, someone would have paid attention at the front end. If liability is imposed in deliberate abstraction from those considerations, why should they play any role in the distribution? Pick any distribution option in between—for example, by designing distribution filters that more or less mimic, but do not require affirmative proof of, individual reliance—and it turns out that deterrence and compensation questions get commingled after all. The soothing assurance that sophisticated statistics and surveys are readily at hand misses the problem. At the tail end of deterrence-first, we no longer have an idea of what it is that we are trying to accomplish.

Double Recoveries

Assume, in the fashion of common economic tort models, a world without transaction costs and without judicial mistakes. And assume that either a common-law regime or deterrence-first rules could yield efficient results. It still does not follow that the conjunction and simultaneous operation of those two regimes will *also* operate efficiently. In real life, though, the regimes do work in tandem. The net result is a regime of double recoveries.

To revert to the case examples, the *Williams* class consists of all OxyContin purchasers for whom the product worked as intended but who claim that it proved addictive, contrary to the company's representations, for some other consumers. Those others are specifically *excluded* from the class and remain free to sue over their alleged injuries regardless of the outcome of the pending *Williams*-style lawsuits. The *Avery* plaintiffs sued on their contracts and under a state consumer-fraud statute. If inferior replacement parts caused consequential damages for some class members (for example, by contributing to a second crash), those individuals remain free to bring suit against the manufacturer, installer, and, presumably, State Farm. The *Price* plaintiffs sued for misrepresentation, not bodily injury; Marlboro Lights smokers in Illinois remain free to bring product-liability lawsuits. Under California's pre-2004 Unfair Competition Law, as noted, verdicts and settlements in cases brought on behalf of the public did not preclude subsequent lawsuits against the same defendants, over the same conduct, by parties who are actually injured by the unlawful conduct (as well as those who are not).

One might say that the lawsuits deter different types of conduct—the sale of a substandard (unsafe, ineffective) product, and fraudulent representations about it. But one cannot easily separate the claims in this fashion. Corporate advertising carries valuable information, and no information whatsoever can be transmitted without some degree of selectivity and, hence, "material omissions" and "misrepresentation." (This is true even where the advertising consists almost exclusively of warnings and disclaimers.[60]) The optimal rule will not seek to eliminate misrepresentation, for that is impossible; it will seek to preserve the informational value while screening out the misrepresentations that induce social losses. That, precisely, is the point of the doctrines of inducement and detrimental reliance: They tie misrepresentation to identifiable harms. Conversely, the defendant's misrepresentations are typically a crucial element in product-liability cases—for example, to defeat the ordinary defenses in contract and tort.

"Deterrence-first" theorists recognize, as they must, that a system that permits both the injured and the uninjured to recover for the full value of the social losses amounts to overcompensation and overdeterrence. Their proposed coordination mechanism is the mandatory class action. But whatever merits that device may have on a blackboard, they do not exist in the real world. What we have are lawsuits of the *Price, Avery,* and *Williams* variety— class actions that conform to the "deterrence-first" model, while preserving product-liability claims.

This dual regime has become very common. For example, voluminous federal and state regulations govern what manufacturers and service-providers may and may not say about pharmaceutical drugs, tobacco products, warranties, equity offerings, credit cards, and mortgage loans. We also have general federal and state prohibitions against "unfair" business practices, which are defined and enforced by the Federal Trade Commission and by state consumer protection agencies. These rules embody rough and ready judgments about the socially acceptable (if not exactly optimal) level of activity. They prohibit conduct that would otherwise have to be deterred by means of litigation. In other words, they are *ex ante* rules in legislative or administrative form. Only rarely, however, do these rules have preclusive and preemptive effect. Marlboro Lights were sold in meticulous compliance with federal laws and regulations governing the labeling and advertising of tobacco products, but that fact failed to impress jurors and judges in Madison County, Illinois.[61] Compliance defenses often fail in liability lawsuits over "unsafe" pharmaceutical drugs or automobiles. And so on. The risk is not simply confusion or incoherence; it is massive overdeterrence.

V

Torts and Statutes

How did we get to the point of entertaining, and compensating, harm-less lawsuits? Undoubtedly, such factors as judicial ideology and modern jurisdictional rules, which allow trial lawyers to file class actions in particularly hospitable forums, have played a role. But it is difficult to account for the phenomenon without considering the crucial role of statutory law. In all the case examples, plaintiffs sued on both statutory and common-law claims, and I seriously doubt that one could find many contemporary class actions of any consequence where a conventional fraud or breach-of-contract claim is *not* accompanied by a statutory claim of unfairness, deception, or misrepresentation. The problems of harm-less lawsuits and double recoveries may stem not so much from private or even class-action litigation *per se*, but from its conjunction or interaction with legislative consumer protections. That observation suggests lessons for both scholars and law reformers.

Law and Politics

The common law may all by itself go off the rails. Multibillion-dollar verdicts in some product-design defect cases are a likely example.[62] Common-law terms and doctrines, from "nuisance" to "unconscionable," and, for that matter, "injury," are sufficiently copious to sustain varying social and economic arrangements under a nominally unchanged doctrine.[63] That openness creates a potential for efficient adaptation—and for ideological flights of fancy. At the end of the day, though, the common law embodies reciprocity relations that are real, not some theoretical construct. Not everything can be a nuisance. My averred right to an unobstructed view is a prohibition on my neighbor's right to expand his home, and that consideration will be obvious to the judge because the defendant will press it with some force. Characterize anything but the literal truth as a "misrepresentation," and all advertising will cease; that intuition explains the continued viability of the distinction between actionable misrepresentation and permissible "puffery." Characterize as "unconscionable" any sales practice or contract terms that might scandalize a middle-class consumer with secure credit (such as a federal judge), and it turns out that sales to low-income, riskier customers dry up altogether.[64] At some level, a common-law judge must care about activity levels as well as harms; about production values as well as consumption; about over- as well as underdeterrence.

So how does one strike a rough balance between those risks? The common-law requirements that circumscribe classes of plaintiffs and actions—much maligned by the consumer-law critique—can be understood as a kind of functional corollary or corrective to the inescapable vagueness of substantive doctrines. For example, a negligent misrepresentation lies somewhere on a spectrum between fraud at one pole and an innocent effort to package consumer information (which can be done only by omitting some stuff that is known to the seller) at the other. In cases alleging misrepresentation, there are substantial costs to erring on either side.

The rough common-law balance is this: On the one hand, the law starts with the recognition that the legal claims that sound in tort—such as fraud—are the third, last line of defense against abuse and exploitation, well after the competitive discipline of the market and contractual arrangements. If the common law of torts underdeters, it does so after the firmer lines of defenses have already been overrun. This does not mean that underdeterrence is an imagined problem. But that risk has to be assessed in its proper, real-world context, where tort law operates alongside more potent protections.

On the other hand, the common law cuts back on inflated loss allegations—which, if given credence, would generate overdeterrence—by limiting the universe of cases to those where the losses are visible with some concreteness. The requirement of detrimental reliance ensures that the plaintiff before the court is actually the marginal consumer, whose losses are far more readily ascertainable than the inframarginal class's estimates of losses to somebody else.

Reciprocity-based inhibitions tend to give way, however, when the legislature signals an intention to promote consumer interests and consumption values. Presumably (the thought or intuition runs), a legislature that enacts a consumer-protection statute wants to do more than to codify preexisting law. Thus, courts may loosen injury requirements and adopt more relaxed notions of inducement and reliance even where the words of the statute leave some doubt about the legislature's intent to prompt that judicial response. Courts, one might say, act on what they take to be the legislature's signals, rather than following its affirmative commands.

This description captures the state judiciaries' response to the enactment of consumer-protection statutes by many states in the 1960s. For the most part, those enactments sought to strengthen the hand of *public* regulators and prosecutors (foremost, the consumer-protection offices of state attorneys general) in enforcing prohibitions against unfair competition, false advertising, and the like.[65] Like the original Federal Trade Commission Act of 1915, analogous state statutes typically grant enforcement agencies broad discretion in defining "unfair" or "deceptive" practices. Generally, public agencies are not required to prove all the common-law elements of statutory offenses (for example, detrimental reliance by individual consumers).[66] This arrangement makes a good deal of sense: Let individual consumers sue over tangible harms, and let public prosecutors—whose abuses can be checked by political and budgetary means—direct their attention to "fraud-on-the-market" offenses that are likely to be underdeterred through private litigation.

Over time, though, many state courts came to read consumer-protection statutes as a warrant for more expansive *private* litigation.[67] The train of thought is not hard to follow; the legislators' enhanced authorization of public prosecutors looks to all eyes like an endorsement of consumer interests outside the confines and strictures of the common law.[68] When private plaintiffs subsequently sue on those more expansive theories, they do not seem to be acting contrary to the statutory intent; to all appearances, they are merely assisting resource-strapped public agencies.

In the 1970s (the heyday of the consumer-law movement), state legislatures made the next move and provided explicitly for the private enforcement of consumer-protection statutes. Most states also provided added incentives for private litigation, typically in the form of attorneys' fees and treble damages for certain violations. While federal courts sought to limit the reach of expansive state statutes (for example, through broad preemption under the Federal Arbitration Act),[69] judicial responses among the states appear to have varied greatly. In some states, courts curtailed what they viewed as excessive private-consumer litigation, often by means of reading common-law requirements of reliance, inducement, and injury into the statutes. In most other states, however, the judiciary accepted the legislature's invitation to give free rein to private enforcers. California provides a particularly dramatic illustration of judicial creativity in expanding the reach of the Unfair Competition Law. Universal private standing under the UCL was a unilateral judicial invention that was neither intended nor anticipated by the legislature.[70]

While the state-by-state differences in institutional agenda-setting and legal development would make an interesting study for political scientists or public-choice theorists,[71] the general theme is the near-uniform tendency toward greatly expanded private-consumer litigation. That tendency is readily explained. In the area of consumer law (as in many other venues), legislatures and courts act as competing suppliers of substantially identical goods. Naturally, the demand for consumer law will gravitate toward the more favorable forum. The default outcome—an expansion of consumer law—will result so long as both *or either* institution says "yes." It can be avoided only if both say "no," or else the naysaying institution affirmatively refuses to cooperate and, moreover, presumes and exercises the authority to rein in its wayward rival. Such a scenario is barely thinkable. Theoretically, state courts could—within the limits of their state constitutions—refuse to apply statutes in derogation of common-law requirements. Theoretically, legislatures could repeal private enforcement provisions or judicial decisions to that effect. Courts and legislatures alike, however, confront great institutional obstacles even in reversing their own decisions, let alone the decisions of a coordinate branch of government.

Long before the enactment of California's Proposition 64 this past November, litigation under the Unfair Competition Law spawned sufficient abuse and distress to prompt stopgap interventions by the office of the attorney general,[72] as well as reform proposals by a law-reform commission that included prominent members of the plaintiffs' bar and by a legal scholar with impeccable consumer-advocacy credentials.[73] Still, the California Supreme Court emphatically declined opportunities to curtail the scope of the statute.[74] The Sacramento legislature, for its part, proved a graveyard for reform proposals. In fact, it repeatedly *expanded* the reach of the UCL, typically in response to limiting judicial rulings.[75] A popular initiative and referendum was the only viable means of breaking the power of entrenched interests and the lamentable logic of institutional deference. California was fortunate to have that option. Many other states, of course, do not.

The Intellectual Agenda

Scholars continue to teach Torts and Contracts without much attention to peripheral interferences from consumer-protection statutes. But the periphery has long begun to overwhelm the common-law center.[76] The widespread failure to acknowledge that reality impedes a forthright, systematic consideration of the central and most challenging tort problem—the conjunction and interaction of disparate theories of enforcement and recovery.

In some settings, redundant and competing systems of law may have considerable benefits. For example, the United States has fifty different systems of corporate law (one in each state), and most scholars believe that this system—relative to a uniform system—

generates useful information about better legal rules and, moreover, reduces the cost and frequency of judicial error. Shareholders and corporate managers sort themselves into one state law regime or another, and each state's law operates to the exclusion of all other states'. Because the parties and their disputes can migrate from one system to another, more suitable one, the systems check each other on the margin. Consumer law and common law, however, do not operate in this competitive sense of "redundancy." They operate jointly and without private opt-outs, and that is bound to compound errors.

To their credit, the most articulate proponents of a deterrence regime (such as professors Fried and Rosenberg) proffer their scheme as an alternative to common-law modes of thought, not as a supplement. They have been at pains to insist that public regulatory schemes are often superior to, and ought to preclude, private litigation.[77] Their clarion call is efficiency, not some transcendental conception of "consumer rights." Precisely the convergence of efficiency theorems and consumerist nostrums, though, ought to give pause—and, after a deep breath, call attention to the difficult task of disentangling and coordinating the conflicting regimes.

Intellectually, the broad contours of such a program are not particularly problematic. The most obvious step is a sharper separation between public and private functions—more precisely, a better alignment of private and public legal forms and instruments with private and public enforcers. While the emphasis on the public (deterrence) function of tort law suggests that the individual plaintiffs and their precise claims are of little consequence, nothing *commands* that inference. Precisely because the law should enhance aggregate social welfare, one could argue, it is hugely important to determine who gets to enforce what. On these grounds, Richard Posner (the principal architect of the "positive" economic theory of tort law) has been very skeptical of broad-based private enforcement. William M. Landes and Posner see nothing sacrosanct in the ownership of common-law claims; rather, they argue that it is extremely difficult to create incentives that will direct private enforcers toward socially beneficial enforcement.[78]

As a rule, we should leave the enforcement of public norms to public enforcers, whose possible proclivities toward overenforcement—unlike the like proclivity of private enforcers—can be checked by political and budgetary means.

Reform?

Consumer-protection statutes have attracted strikingly little attention not only in the scholarly literature but also in the public and political debate over "tort reform." (The term itself suggests the lack of attention to statutory law.) The business community—obviously, the constituency with the biggest stake—has largely failed to focus on the central role of consumer statutes, their private enforcement, and their interaction with (greatly expanded) common-law liability doctrines. Perhaps that is so because billion-dollar verdicts in "misrepresentation" cases are of somewhat more recent vintage than older, equally spectacular product-liability cases. Perhaps collective-action problems impede a concerted effort. The business community may prefer a unifying agenda—such as a campaign against punitive damages, which every corporation opposes—to an agenda that would require a partial surrender of tactical opportunities. The corporate plaintiffs in *Desanio*, for example, understandably care more about their $1.4 billion demand than about some abstract tort-reform proposals.

California's Proposition 64 embodies the policy urged here: Restrict private enforcement to actually harmed consumers, and commit the enforcement of public norms of acceptable business conduct to public agencies. Its trajectory illustrates both the force of such short-sighted business calculations and the possibility of overcoming them. The universal-standing rule of California's Section 17200 permitted not only consumers but also business firms to sue their competitors, and firms routinely availed themselves of that opportunity. In one much-noted case, AIG sued a competing insurance firm for defrauding its—the competitor's—own policyholders. AIG sued not to redress a harm to itself, but rather for the benefit of raising its rival's cost of doing business.[79] Ultimately, though, the legal environment became sufficiently intolerable to unite business behind a reform—Proposition 64—that promised long-term collective gains in excess of short-term gains (or "rents," as economists say). That agreement was neither easy nor cost-free, but it did eventually materialize.

The fact that Proposition 64 had to be enacted through a popular referendum rather than ordinary legislation suggests that the major impediments to a pragmatic reform program may lie on the political supply side, rather than the demand side. State and federal legislators pay scant attention to the effects of private litigation under consumer-protection statutes because they have an incentive to pretend that the "liability crisis" is altogether the fault of an out-of-control judiciary. Barring a clear legislative signal, judges have no incentive to curtail the private enforcement of public-law norms against misrepresentation and the like. State attorneys general, for their part, do not jealously guard their prerogative to enforce public norms.[80] To the contrary, they are closely allied with the trial bar, and their investigations often serve to drive down the discovery costs for class-action lawyers (who kick back a portion of the windfall in the form of campaign contributions). Legal arrangements not only result from but also generate interest group support. The loosening of common-law requirements in the 1970s had the intended result of facilitating consumer litigation by public-interest organizations and legal-aid groups.[81] Those groups continue to operate, but their dominance over consumer litigation has proved temporary. Consumer law now responds to the demands of lone rangers (like Marc Kasky) and, far more importantly, the class-action bar.

What makes these constituencies flourish is precisely the bizarre interplay of public- and private-law arguments, or perhaps better tropes. Tell a class-action lawyer that damages for claims without injury or reliance interests are a dramatic departure from common-law norms; the answer is that such actions provide vital assistance to resource-strapped public prosecutors in enforcing public norms. Argue that the private pursuit of public purposes (here, deterrence) precludes nonpecuniary damages, or that a public-safety standard—a rough-and-ready judgment about the acceptable deterrence level—ought by all rights to preclude private design-defect lawsuits over products that satisfy the standard; the answer is that public agencies are captured and corrupt and that, in any event, everyone deserves his day in court.[82]

If neither of these responses strikes ordinary Americans as obviously crazy, that is because neither—in isolation—*is* crazy. The problem, to repeat, lies in the conjunction. There is something admirable about the rigorous effort to construct efficient deterrence norms in isolation from the vagaries of individualized common-law adjudication, and something refreshingly candid about the readiness with which leading proponents of that view— prominently, David Rosenberg—denounce notions of plaintiff autonomy and the individual's right to a day in court as so much sentimental nonsense and as an invitation to *ex post* opportunism.[83] The catch is the real world, where the sentimentalists and opportunists will continue to vote and litigate and agitate in defiance of elegant schemes, especially in a culture where common-law modes of thought continue to exert a powerful pull.

The trial bar (and its consumer group and attorney-general pilot fish) thrive on that ambiguity. They solemnly insist on the right of the least among us to have their day in court, even while seizing on the public-law versions of law and economics scholarship. They can live very profitably in two legal worlds at once. The productive sectors of American society pay the price for that comfort. That insight should prompt a realistic estimation of the nature of the problem—and, hopefully, more serious intellectual and political efforts to address it.

Notes

1. *Price v. Philip Morris*, Circuit Court Madison County, Ill., Case No. 00-L-112 (March 21, 2003) (Byron, J.), http://www.altria.com/download/pdf/Miles_Judgement_21March03.pdf (accessed February 8, 2005). The case is discussed on page 21.

2. The point is explained on pages 18 and 19. I will sacrifice precision to convenience and refer to "harm-less lawsuits" or "lawsuits without injuries."

3. For an exhaustive, penetrating account of this transformation, see George L. Priest in "The Invention of Enterprise Liability: A Critical History of the Intellectual Foundations of Modern Tort Law," *Journal of Legal Studies* 14 (1985): 461–533.

4. *In re Bridgestone/Firestone Inc.*, 288 F3d 1012, 1017 (7th Cir. 2002) (Easterbrook, J.).

5. Judge Frank H. Easterbrook credits the observation to former University of Chicago Law School Dean Gerhard Casper, who—for the sorts of reasons suggested in the text—was proud that his institution did not offer a course in "the law of the horse." Easterbrook, "Cyberspace and the Law of the Horse," *University of Chicago Legal Forum* (1996): 207–16.

6. For a general treatment and an emphatic defense of common-law instruments, see Richard A. Epstein, *Forbidden Grounds: The Case against Employment Discrimination Laws* (Boston: Harvard University Press, 1992).

7. See, for example, Frederick H. Miller, Alvin C. Harrell, and Daniel J. Morgan, *Consumer Law: Cases, Problems, and Materials* (Durham: Carolina Academic Press, 1998), 3, and Michael M. Greenfield, *Consumer Law: A Guide for Those Who Represent Sellers, Lenders, and Consumers* (Boston: Little, Brown and Company, 1995), 2.

8. Even casebooks display that tendency: "[In consumer transactions,] the position of the parties is such that the consumer is faced with a take-it-or-leave-it proposition, and often few alternative sources of supply

offering any substantially different deal." Miller et al., *Consumer Law: Cases, Problems and Materials*, 4.

9. The "crude and crackpot" designation applies foremost to Friedrich Kessler, whose pathbreaking contributions rested on the notion that consumer contracts—under modern conditions of mass production—are an instrument of fascist social control. For a judicious discussion of Kessler's momentous influence, see Priest, "The Invention of Enterprise Liability," 484–96. For an intriguing discussion of the modern, more empirically based scholarship, see Jon D. Hanson and Douglas A. Kysar, "Taking Behavioralism Seriously: The Problem of Market Manipulation," *New York University Law Review* 74 (1999): 630–749.

10. Colin Camerer, Samuel Issacharoff, George Loewenstein, Ted O'Donoghue, and Matthew Rabin, "Regulation for Conservatives: Behavioral Economics and the Case for 'Asymmetric Paternalism,'" *University of Pennsylvania Law Review* 151 (2003): 1211–54. The regulatory strategies that flow from this rationale are often orthogonal to existing, well-nigh sacrosanct, consumer protections. Disclosure obligations for public corporations and broker-dealers, for example, are touted as protections for the proverbial "small investor." But if equity markets are even approximately efficient, the vast majority of those investors should not dabble in the market; they should buy index funds. By taking those investors as the yardstick, disclosure regulation may create a moral hazard, while distorting or suppressing information (such as forward-looking information) that would be of use to more sophisticated investors. Arguably, an efficient paternalistic regime would license stock buyers, not brokers. See Stephen J. Choi and Andrew T. Guzman, "Portable Reciprocity: Rethinking the International Reach of Securities Regulation," *Southern California Law Review* 71 (1998): 942–43.

11. See, for example, Abram Chayes, "The Role of the Judge in Public Law Litigation," *Harvard Law Review* 89 (1976): 1281–1316; Owen Fiss, "The Supreme Court, 1978 Term—The Forms of Justice," *Harvard Law Review* 93 (1979): 1–58; Ronald Dworkin, *Law's Empire* (Boston: Harvard University Press, 1986); and Cass R. Sunstein, "Beyond the Republican Revival," *Yale Law Journal* 97 (1988): 1539–90. For a trenchant critique, see Jeremy A. Rabkin, *Judicial Compulsions* (New York: Basic Books, 1989).

12. Brian Mannix, "The Origin of Endangered Species and the Descent of Man," *The American Enterprise* 3, no. 6 (November/December 1992): 56–63. For the continued appearance of this ecological paradigm in the case law see, for example, *National Association of Home Builders v. Babbitt*, 130 F3d 1041, 1052–54 (D.C. Cir. 1997) (Wald, J.), holding that the federal

Endangered Species Act passes constitutional muster under the Commerce Clause due to the interconnectedness of the world. For a fuller discussion and critique of the ecological perspective, see Michael S. Greve, *The Demise of Environmentalism in American Law* (Washington, D.C.: AEI Press, 1996).

13. See Samuel Issacharoff, "Governance and Legitimacy in the Law of Class Actions," *Supreme Court Review* (1999): 345, and John C. Coffee, "Class Action Accountability: Reconciling Exit, Voice, and Loyalty in Representative Legislation," *Columbia Law Review* 100 (2000): 371n1.

14. The literature on banking and consumer loan regulation has amply documented the phenomenon. See, for example, Christopher C. DeMuth, "The Case Against Credit Card Interest Regulation," *Yale Journal of Regulation* 3 (1986): 201–41, and Todd Zywicki, "The Economics of Credit Cards," *Chapman Law Review* 3 (2000): 79–172. In the area of subprime mortgage lending, consumer advocates are pressing—at both the state and the federal level—for the regulation of opaque loan terms whose use was very likely induced by earlier rounds of "consumer protection" legislation, in particular *de facto* usury ceilings. See Michael S. Greve, "Subprime, But Not Half-Bad: Mortgage Regulation as a Case Study in Preemption," *Federalist Outlook* No. 19 (Washington, D.C.: American Enterprise Institute, September–October 2003), http://www.aei.org/publications/filter.,pubID.19271/pub_detail.asp (accessed January 19, 2005).

15. David Rosenberg, "The Causal Connection in Mass Exposure Cases: A 'Public Law' Vision of the Tort System," *Harvard Law Review* 97 (1984): 849–929.

16. See, for example, Paul H. Rubin, *Tort Reform by Contract* (Washington, D.C.: AEI Press, 1993); Richard A. Epstein, "The Legal and Insurance Dynamics of Mass Tort Litigation," *Journal of Legal Studies* 13 (1984): 475–506; and George Priest, "The Current Insurance Crisis and Modern Tort Law," *Yale Law Journal* 96 (1987): 1521–90.

17. Charles Fried and David Rosenberg, *Making Tort Law: What Should Be Done and Who Should Do It* (Washington, D.C.: AEI Press, 2003).

18. Ibid., 13–26. The designation of deterrence as an "insurance" function is a bit misleading because optimal deterrence will also seek to induce efficient investments to avoid harms—such as loss of an infant child—which rational consumers will *not* insure. See page 15.

19. For example, the administrative costs of workmen's compensation—no one's idea of efficient insurance—are approximately 23 percent of total costs. In contrast, upward of 58 percent of tort costs consist of lawyers' fees

and other transaction costs. Council of Economic Advisers, *Who Pays for Tort Liability Claims? An Economic Analysis of the U.S. Tort Liability System* (Washington, D.C.: April 2002), 9–10, http://www.whitehouse.gov/cea/tortliabilitysystem_apr02.pdf (accessed January 18, 2005).

20. The crucial assumption here is that it is possible to determine optimal deterrence without taking the plaintiffs' conduct into account. But that is not obviously correct. If A knows that B is in error, should liability attach nonetheless for B's misrepresentation—or should A be required to alter its behavior? For an example illustrating the potential significance of this point, see pages 29–30.

21. David Rosenberg, "Decoupling Deterrence and Compensation Functions in Mass Tort Class Actions for Future Loss," *Virginia Law Review* 88 (2002): 1871–1919.

22. David Rosenberg, "Mandatory-Litigation Class Action: The Only Option for Mass Tort Cases," *Harvard Law Review* 115 (2002): 831–97. See also Rosenberg, "Decoupling Deterrence and Compensation," 1912, where he writes that class-action opt-out on grounds of plaintiff autonomy "is a prescription for making everyone worse off."

23. James Buchanan and Gordon Tullock, *The Calculus of Consent* (Ann Arbor, Mich.: University of Michigan Press, 1962); John Rawls, *A Theory of Justice* (Cambridge, Mass.: Harvard University Press, 1971).

24. Richard Posner, *An Economic Analysis of Law*, 5th ed. (New York: Aspen, 1998), 105.

25. For a defense of this model and its implications for class actions, see Richard A. Epstein, "Class Actions: Aggregation, Amplification and Distortion," *University of Chicago Legal Forum* (2003): 475–517.

26. A notable exception to this general practice is Steven Shavell, "A Model of the Optimal Use of Liability and Safety Regulation," *RAND Journal of Economics* 15 (1984): 271–80.

27. See, for example, William Landes and Richard Posner, *The Economic Structure of Tort Law* (Cambridge, Mass.: Harvard University Press, 1987), 1. The alternative view, which is much more consonant with common-law intuitions, is to view tort law as being shaped primarily by *litigants* rather than judges. The pathbreaking contribution in this vein is Paul H. Rubin, "Common Law and Statute Law," *Journal of Legal Studies* 11 (1982): 205–24. From this vantage, who gets to sue and precisely for what matter immensely.

28. The classic exposition of modern tort law as an efficient response to urbanization and the increased distance from consumers to producers is William M. Landes and Richard A. Posner, "A Positive Economic Analysis of

Products Liability," *Journal of Legal Studies* 14 (1985): 535–67. See also Landes and Posner, *The Economic Structure of Tort Law*, 284–85; and Steven Shavell, *The Economics of Accident Law* (Cambridge, Mass.: Harvard University Press, 1987), 54. For references to the burgeoning behavioralist literature on consumer biases, see notes 9 and 10 above.

29. See note 19, above.

30. For a thorough discussion, see John E. Calfee and Paul H. Rubin, "Some Implications of Damage Payments for Nonpecuniary Losses," *Journal of Legal Studies* 21 (1992): 371–411.

31. Robert D. Cooter and Daniel L. Rubinfeld, "Economic Analysis of Legal Disputes and Their Resolution," *Journal of Economic Literature* 27 (1989): 1094. Reprinted in Richard A. Posner and Francesco Parisi, eds., *Economic Foundations of Private Law* (Northampton, Mass.: Edward Elger Publishing, 2002), 173–203.

32. Don Dewees, David Duff, and Michael Trebilcock, *Exploring the Domain of Accident Law: Taking the Facts Seriously* (Oxford: Oxford University Press, 1996), 414.

33. *Shaw v. Toshiba America Information Systems Inc.*, 91 F. Supp. 2d 926 (E.D. Tex. 1999); Andy Pasztor and Peter Landers, "Toshiba to Pay $2B Settlement on Laptops," ZDNet.com, October 31, 1999, http://zdnet.com.com/2100-11-516294.html (accessed February 8, 2005).

34. Michael Kelly, "The Phantom Reliant Interest in Tort Damages," *San Diego Law Review* 38 (2001): 170–71. See also *Restatement (Second) of Torts* § 549 cmt. g (criticizing the practice but acknowledging its preponderance).

35. Suppose a ruthless operator sells an ointment on the false promise that it will absolutely, positively rid users of cellulite. Under the traditional rule, the appropriate liability award is the purchase price plus consequential damages and opportunity costs, if any. Benefit-of-the-bargain redress means the difference between the purchase price and the benefits buyers would have derived from an actually effective (though regrettably nonexistent) cellulite cure. If the stuff were peddled to a class of desperate housewives, the sum could be very large—unless the court pays close attention to the reliance requirement. It is, of course, impossible to estimate the difference in value between a quack remedy and a nonexistent product, but that consideration has not always deterred courts from awarding benefit-of-the-bargain redress in comparable cases. See the discussion of *Price v. Philip Morris*, page 21. The ointment hypothetical is loosely based on a case that was the subject of a Federal Trade Commission proceeding and two separate class actions. See

FTC v. Rexall Sundown, Inc., "Stipulated Final Order for Permanent Injunction and Settlement of Claims for Monetary Relief," http://www.ftc.gov/os/2003/03/rexallstiporder.htm (accessed January 19, 2005). Redress in that settlement was limited to the estimated purchase price.

36. The consumer surplus is the difference between the price consumers paid for a given product and the highest price that they would have been prepared to pay.

37. 297 F. Supp. 2d 171 (D.D.C. 2003).

38. An appellate court subsequently reduced the judgment by $130 million. *Avery v. State Farm*, 321 Ill. App. 3d 269, 746 N.E. 2d 1242 (Ill. App. Ct. 2001). The case is pending on an appeal to the Illinois Supreme Court.

39. A federal district court had dismissed the complaint; the Second Circuit Court of Appeals reinstated it. *Desanio v. Warner-Lambert Co.*, 326 F.3d 339 (2nd Cir. 2003).

40. The nationwide class certified in *Avery v. State Farm* is problematic in many respects. It could not possibly be sustained in the Seventh Circuit, which covers Illinois. See *In re Firestone/Bridgestone*, 288 F.3d 1012 (7th Cir. 2002), rehearing *en banc* denied, 288 F.3d 1012 (7th Cir. 2002), *cert. denied*, 537 U.S. 1105 (2003). Due to the requirement of complete diversity, however, the case could not be removed to federal court. State Farm's repeated attempts to have the class decertified in state court and through an interlocutory petition for certiorari to the U.S. Supreme Court were unsuccessful.

41. *Shaw v. Toshiba*, 91 F. Supp. 2d 926, 938 (footnote omitted; emphasis in original), 941.

42. *Stop Youth Addiction v. Lucky Stores*, 17 Cal. 4th 553 (1998). In fact, the law need not be a California law. See *Schwartz v. Upper Deck Co.*, 967 F. Supp. 405 (S.D. Cal. 1997) (explicitly holding that alleged violations of federal RICO law can serve as a predicate for lawsuit under the UCL).

43. James R. McCall, Patricia Sturdevant, Laura Kaplan, and Gail Hillebrand, "Greater Representation for California Consumers—Fluid Recovery, Consumer Trust Funds, and Representative Actions," *Hastings Law Journal* 46 (1995): 822–25.

44. *Podolsky v. First Healthcare Corp.*, 50 Cal. App. 4th 632, 647–48 (1996), citing *State Farm v. Superior Court*, 45 Cal. App. 4th 1093 (1996); and *Committee on Children's Television v. General Foods Corp.*, 35 Cal. 3d 197 (1983).

45. See, for example, *Consumers Union of the United States Inc. v. Fisher Development Inc.*, 208 Cal. App. 3d 1443, 1440 (1989); and *Stop Youth Addiction v. Lucky Stores*, 17 Cal. 4th 553, 565 (1998).

46. Gail E. Lees, "The Defense of Private and Governmental Unfair Competition Law Claims," *Unfair Competition Claims 2003: California Section 17200's Impact on Consumers & Businesses Everywhere*, Practicing Law Institute Litigation and Administrative Practice Course Handbook Series 694 (2003), 306. For a brief overview of the available forms of relief, see McCall et al., "Greater Representation for California Consumers," 826–49.

47. *Kasky v. Nike*, 27 Cal. 4th 939, 45 P.3d 243, 119 Cal. Rptr. 2d 296 (2002); *Nike v. Kasky*, 123 S. Ct. 2554 (2003). For a description of the settlement see http://www.nike.com/nikebiz/news/pressrelease.jhtml?year=2003& month=09&letter=f, (accessed January 19, 2005).

48. Cass Sunstein has repeatedly urged the mobilization of "public law" for a "republican discourse." See Sunstein, *Democracy and the Problem of Free Speech* (New York: Free Press, 1993): 39–43, 68–92. Mercifully, Sunstein shrinks from the practical implications of his proposal. See Stephen F. Williams, "Background Norms in the Regulatory State," *University of Chicago Law Review* 58 (1991): 427–29. More practical-minded individuals like Marc Kasky lack such inhibitions.

49. See, for example, *Bronco Wine Co. v. Frank A. Lugoso Farms*, 214 Cal. App. 3d 699, 720 (1989): "One must question the utility of a procedure that results in a judgment that is not binding on the nonparty and has serious and fundamental due process deficiencies for the parties and nonparties." In a *dictum* in *Kraus v. Trinity Mgmt. Serv. Inc.*, 23 Cal. 4th 116, 138–39 (2000), the California Supreme Court suggested that courts might tackle the possibility of future suits by "condition[ing] payment of restitution . . . on execution of acknowledgement that the payment is in full settlement of claims against the defendant, thereby avoiding any potential for repetitive suits on behalf of the same persons or dual liability to them." Such an extrastatutory band-aid, however, would do nothing to preclude follow-on suits in cases where the defendant prevailed in the first case. Moreover, it would do nothing to prevent plaintiffs' lawyer from disposing of the claims of members of the public, including actually injured parties, without any of the formal and due-process protection of a class action.

50. This proposition holds as a matter of theory. In practice, opportunistic claims and judicial error will often deplete the pool. See pages 27–33.

51. Rosenberg, "Decoupling Deterrence and Compensation," 1896.

52. See McCall et al., "Greater Representation for California Consumers," 848.

53. Rosenberg, "Decoupling Deterrence and Compensation," 1893.

54. *Avery v. State Farm*, 746 N.E. 2d 1242, 1260 (Ill. 2001). The court nonetheless characterized the expert's testimony as more than "sheer speculation." 746 N.E. 2d at 1261.

55. Arguably, a counterfactual scenario is available in the case of cigarettes. There are good reasons to believe that smokers are fully cognizant of the risks and, if anything, overestimate them. Kip Viscusi, *Smoking: Making the Risky Decision* (New York: Oxford University Press, 1992), 87–117. The notion that smokers are shocked—shocked!—to learn that lights are not actually safe is too inane to be believed by anyone—except an Illinois court.

56. Suppose that companies will provide information to the brokers' analysts only if the brokers agree to issue a recommendation no lower than "hold." (The information will otherwise be limited to insiders.) And suppose that investors can cross-check the brokers' recommendations at almost no cost against independent sources (such as by taking a quick look at Value Line, available at the local library). The infliction of liability would almost certainly induce a social loss.

57. *In re Merrill Lynch*, 273 F. Supp. 2d 351 (S.D.N.Y. 2003).

58. Suppose we decide to discount the deterrence award by the same ratio by which investors discounted the brokers' hype *ex ante*. What is that ratio?

59. For a thoughtful presentation of this point and its implications, see Francis E. McGovern, "The What and Why of Claims Resolution Facilities," *Stanford Law Review* (forthcoming).

60. Consider the television ads for certain pharmaceutical products: As Mr. and Mrs. "Sixty-Is-the-New-Forty" gallivant through the daisies, the FDA-mandated voiceover recites a litany of possible afflictions that should make all but the compulsive see sex in a whole new light—except for the warning that "erections lasting more than a few hours require medical attention."

61. Defendants' preemption argument was rejected by the court. *Price v. Philip Morris*, No. 00-L-112, 2003 WL 22597608 at 19, ¶111 (Ill. Cir. 2003) (rejecting defendants' claim under the Federal Cigarette Advertising and Labeling Act, 15 U.S.C. 133 et seq.).

62. See, for example, *Anderson v. General Motors Corp.*, No. BC-116926 (Cal. Super. Ct., Los Angeles County 1999). The fuel tank of Anderson's 1979 Chevy Malibu burst into flames after her car was rear-ended by a drunk driver. The jury found GM responsible and awarded $4.9 billion in damages. The figure was later reduced to $1.2 billion.

63. The textbook example is still Judge Skelly Wright's wholesale transformation of "unconscionability" in *Williams v. Walker-Thomas Furniture*, 350 F.2d 445 (D.C. Cir. 1965).

64. See Richard A. Epstein, "Unconscionability: A Critical Reappraisal," *Journal of Law and Economics* 18 (1975): 293–315.

65. For an overview and critical appraisal, see Jeff Sovern, "Private Actions under the Deceptive Trade Practices Act: Reconsidering the FTC Act as a Rule Model," *Ohio State Law Journal* 52 (1991): 437–67.

66. Agencies need not even allege or show that a "misrepresentation" was false. See, for example, *Bockenstette v. FTC*, 134 F.2d 369, 371 (10th Cir. 1943): "It is not necessary . . . for the Commission to find that actual deception resulted"; *FTC v. Balme*, 23 F.2d 615, 621 (2nd Cir. 1928): "Nor is it necessary . . . to find . . . that any competitor of the respondent has been damaged"; *FTC v. Sterling Drugs*, 317 F.2d 669, 674 (2nd Cir. 1963): "Proof of intention to deceive is not requisite to a finding of violation of the statute."

67. Seth William Goren, "A Pothole on the Road to Recovery: Reliance and Private Class Actions under Pennsylvania's Unfair Trade Practices and Consumer Protection Law," *Dickinson Law Review* 107 (2002): 13–14nn50–51.

68. For a random example, see *Creamer ex rel. Commonwealth v. Monumental Properties Inc.*, 329 A.2d 812, 822 (Pa. 1974): "We cannot presume that the Legislature when attempting to control unfair and deceptive practices . . . intended to be strictly bound by common-law formalisms. Rather the more natural inference is that the Legislature intended the Consumer Protection Law to be given a pragmatic reading."

69. See *Southland Corp. v. Keating*, 465 U.S. 1, 16 (1984) and *Allied-Bruce Terminix Cos. v. Dobson*, 513 U.S. 265, 281 (1995). For other examples of federal judicial hostility to liberal state-pleading and standing rules, see *Bullet Golf Inc. v. United States Golf Ass'n*, 1995 U.S. Dist. LEXIS 6189, at *2 (C.D. Cal. March 20, 1995), dismissing a claim under California law for lack of credible allegation of actual deception and injury; and *Williams v. Purdue Pharma Co.*, 297 F. Supp. 2d 171, 174, 177 (D.D.C. 2003), dismissing a consumer complaint for lack of injury despite statutory language authorizing "any person" to seek redress for illegal trade practices.

70. The universal-standing decision is *Barquis v. Merchants Collection Association of Oakland Inc.*, 496 P.2d 817 (1972). The statutory text and legislative history of the UCL are discussed in *Stop Youth Addiction v. Lucky Stores*, 950 P.2d 1086, 1107–9 (1998) (Brown, J., dissenting).

71. See Paul Rubin, "Public Choice and Tort Reform," http://papers. ssrn.com/sol3/papers.cfm?abstract_id=575741 (accessed January 19, 2005).

72. Attorney General Bill Lockyer filed suit against a Beverly Hills law firm under the same Unfair Competition Law that the firm was accused of abus-

ing. See "Attorney General Lockyer Files '17200' Consumer Protection Lawsuit against Beverly Hills Law Firm," press release, February 26, 2003, http://caag.state.ca.us/newsalerts/2003/03-021.htm (accessed January 18, 2005).

73. California Law Revision Commission, "Recommendation: Unfair Competition Litigation," November 1996, http://www.clrc.ca.gov/pub/ Printed-Reports/Pub191-UnfairComp.pdf (accessed January 18, 2005); Robert Fellmeth, "Unfair Competition Act Enforcement by Agencies, Prosecutors, and Private Litigants: Who's on First?" *California Regulatory Law Reporter* 15 (Winter, 1995): 1–11.

74. See, for example, *Stop Youth Addiction v. Lucky Stores*, 17 Cal. 4th 553, 597 (Cal. 1998) (Brown, J., dissenting), observing that "the Courts of Appeal have done an admirable job of reining in the UCL's potential for adverse regulatory effects" and charging majority with "choos[ing] to speed us along the path to perdition."

75. See, for example, Cal. Bus. & Prof. Code § 17203, as amended by S.B. 1586 (1992 Cal. Stat. Ch. 430, § 3), reversing *Mangini v. Aerojet-General Corp.*, 230 Cal. App. 3d (1991), which had held that UCL provides injunctive relief only for ongoing but not past violations; and SB 1586 (1992 Cal. Stat. Ch. 430, § 2), reversing *California v. Texaco Inc.*, 46 Cal. 3d 1147 (1988) and clarifying that UCL applies to individual business "acts" as well as practices.

76. Stewart Macauly, "Bambi Meets Godzilla: Reflections on Contracts Scholarship and Teaching v. State Unfair Practices and Consumer Protection Statutes," *Houston Law Review* 26 (1989): 575–76.

77. Fried and Rosenberg, *Making Tort Law*, 14: "Crucially, *ex ante* and *ex post* preferences are mutually exclusive concerning the fundamental purpose of the legal system in managing accident risk," and generally 66–102; Rosenberg, "Decoupling Deterrence and Compensation," 1918–19.

78. The ingenious argument (obvious, once it has been stated) appears in William M. Landes and Richard Posner, "The Private Enforcement of Law," *Journal of Legal Studies* 4 (1975): 1.

79. AIG initiated the California suit in 1999, after the Pennsylvania Supreme Court had tossed out the company's identical suit. Bernard Condon, "Ace in the Hole," Forbes.com, August 11, 2003, http://www.forbes.com/forbes/2003/0811/040_print.html (accessed January 19, 2005). After five years of litigation, the California case is still pending. The question of whether Proposition 64, which would very likely bar AIG's lawsuit, applies to pending cases is unresolved.

80. For example, California Attorney General Bill Lockyer strenuously opposed Proposition 64 and has expressed dismay over its enactment. See Carolyn Whetzel, "California Voters Approve Initiative to Limit Private Actions Enforcing Competition Laws," *Bureau of National Affairs Daily Report for Executives* 213 (November 4, 2004): B1.

81. Macauly, "Bambi Meets Godzilla," 583.

82. Even environmentalists are now supplementing their long-held public-law conceptions with private-law remedies—as when state attorneys general, on behalf of their citizens, sue utilities over their carbon-dioxide emissions, not under the Clean Air Act but rather under a common-law theory of nuisance (which happens to affect the entire planet). See Jonathan H. Adler, "Heated Nuisance Suits," TechCentralStation.com, July 27, 2004, http://www.techcentralstation.com/072704C.html (accessed January 19, 2005).

83. Rosenberg, "Decoupling Deterrence and Compensation," 1911–16.

About the Author

Michael S. Greve is the John G. Searle Scholar at the American Enterprise Institute in Washington, D.C., where he directs the AEI Federalism Project and the AEI Liability Project. His research and writing cover American federalism and its legal, political, and economic dimensions.

Mr. Greve cofounded and, from 1989 to 2000, directed the Center for Individual Rights (CIR), a public interest law firm. CIR served as counsel in many precedent-setting constitutional cases, including *United States v. Morrison* (2000) and *Rosenberger v. University of Virginia* (1995). He currently serves on the board of directors of the Competitive Enterprise Institute.

Mr. Greve earned his PhD in government from Cornell University in 1987. He is the editor, with Fred L. Smith, of *Environmental Politics: Public Costs, Private Rewards* (Praeger, 1992); and the author of *The Demise of Environmentalism in American Law* (AEI Press, 1996), *Real Federalism: Why It Matters, How It Could Happen* (AEI Press, 1999), and *Sell Globally, Tax Locally: Sales Tax Reform for the New Economy* (AEI Press, 2003). Mr. Greve is also the coeditor, with Richard A. Epstein, of *Competition Laws in Conflict: Antitrust Jurisdiction in the Global Economy* (AEI Press, 2004).

Jeremy Rabkin
Professor of Government
Cornell University

Murray L. Weidenbaum
Mallinckrodt Distinguished
University Professor
Washington University

Richard J. Zeckhauser
Frank Plumpton Ramsey Professor
of Political Economy
Kennedy School of Government
Harvard University

Research Staff

Joseph Antos
Wilson H. Taylor Scholar in Health
Care and Retirement Policy

Leon Aron
Resident Scholar

Claude E. Barfield
Resident Scholar; Director, Science
and Technology Policy Studies

Roger Bate
Resident Fellow

Walter Berns
Resident Scholar

Douglas J. Besharov
Joseph J. and Violet Jacobs
Scholar in Social Welfare Studies

Daniel Blumenthal
Resident Fellow

Karlyn H. Bowman
Resident Fellow

John E. Calfee
Resident Scholar

Charles W. Calomiris
Arthur F. Burns Scholar in
Economics

Lynne V. Cheney
Senior Fellow

Veronique de Rugy
Research Fellow

Thomas Donnelly
Resident Fellow

Nicholas Eberstadt
Henry Wendt Scholar in Political
Economy

Eric M. Engen
Resident Scholar

Mark Falcoff
Resident Scholar Emeritus

Gerald R. Ford
Distinguished Fellow

John C. Fortier
Research Fellow

David Frum
Resident Fellow

Ted Gayer
Visiting Scholar

Reuel Marc Gerecht
Resident Fellow

Newt Gingrich
Senior Fellow

James K. Glassman
Resident Fellow

Jack L. Goldsmith
Visiting Scholar

Robert A. Goldwin
Resident Scholar

Scott Gottlieb
Resident Fellow

Michael S. Greve
John G. Searle Scholar

Robert W. Hahn
Resident Scholar; Director,
AEI-Brookings Joint Center
for Regulatory Studies

Kevin A. Hassett
Resident Scholar; Director,
Economic Policy Studies

Steven F. Hayward
F. K. Weyerhaeuser Fellow

Robert B. Helms
Resident Scholar; Director,
Health Policy Studies

Frederick M. Hess
Resident Scholar; Director,
Education Policy Studies

R. Glenn Hubbard
Visiting Scholar

Leon R. Kass
Hertog Fellow

Jeane J. Kirkpatrick
Senior Fellow

Herbert G. Klein
National Fellow

Marvin H. Kosters
Resident Scholar

Irving Kristol
Senior Fellow

Randall S. Kroszner
Visiting Scholar

Desmond Lachman
Resident Fellow

Michael A. Ledeen
Freedom Scholar

James R. Lilley
Senior Fellow

Lawrence B. Lindsey
Visiting Scholar

John R. Lott Jr.
Resident Scholar

John H. Makin
Visiting Scholar

Allan H. Meltzer
Visiting Scholar

Hedieh Mirahmadi
Visiting Scholar

Joshua Muravchik
Resident Scholar

Charles Murray
W. H. Brady Scholar

Michael Novak
George Frederick Jewett Scholar
in Religion, Philosophy, and Public
Policy; Director, Social and Political
Studies

Norman J. Ornstein
Resident Scholar

Richard Perle
Resident Fellow

Alex J. Pollock
Resident Fellow

Sarath Rajapatirana
Visiting Scholar

Michael Rubin
Resident Scholar

Sally Satel
Resident Scholar

Joel Schwartz
Visiting Fellow

Daniel Shaviro
Visiting Scholar

J. Gregory Sidak
Resident Scholar

Radek Sikorski
Resident Fellow; Executive
Director, New Atlantic Initiative

Christina Hoff Sommers
Resident Scholar

Phillip Swagel
Resident Scholar

Samuel Thernstrom
Managing Editor, AEI Press;
Director, W. H. Brady Program

Fred Thompson
Visiting Fellow

Peter J. Wallison
Resident Fellow

Scott Wallsten
Resident Scholar

Ben J. Wattenberg
Senior Fellow

John Yoo
Visiting Fellow

Karl Zinsmeister
J. B. Fuqua Fellow; Editor,
The American Enterprise